Subsidence
R.M. Francis

smoke

STACK
BOOKS

Smokestack Books
1 Lake Terrace, Grewelthorpe,
Ripon HG4 3BU
e-mail: info@smokestack-books.co.uk
www.smokestack-books.co.uk

ISBN 9781916312111

Smokestack Books
is represented by
Inpress Ltd

Contents

Wieland I

'E knows 'ow to kip a furnace burnin'
through days an' nights a sun an' snow.
Alruna gid 'im the runes for churnin',
'e knows 'ow to kip a furnace burnin.

Gram-sword deft kept knights returnin' –
'e toils dirt-ore to whetted-glow.
'E knows 'ow to kip a furnace burnin'
through days an' nights a sun an' snow.

Peering

The buildings, stained by industry tears,
scar those passing through.
They wallow in rancid reflections of filthy windows
and get caught – anaesthetised.
They flee, but I like the dry-eyed, dirty face
peering back behind the advertisements.

Burning Tongues

We ay from brumajum
weem in the borderless
pits – black be day
red be night. Where baby
rhymes with Rabbie – that old
bard who kept the burn
in his tongue.
That burn connects, it burns
like our old forges burned –
burning trade and toil and song
and burning a brand
that yow know and yow know –
burns like Saxon shamans
who's embers were stamped
and pissed on by ministers
of education immersed in
double spayke –
thass why weem taught
to hayte those four letter words
like fuck and cunt.
Those words burn and words
that burn sit, like us,
in borderless pits, ready,
with Blakean bows, to fight
shot to shot – to burn back
with our vernacular,
thass why when my Auntie
sez *yow doh spayke proper* 'er's
playing 'er part in burning.

Two Wenches Contemplate the Langue

'Could've been that Tomo, e's' a cunt?'
It began between two callused wenches
Suppin' halves an' cantin'
'Well, crack heads am the wust,
I got one today, 'e was alright … Iraqi'.

'Iraqi?'
Each word spat out to each, cantin'
bitter thoughts between two bitter wenches
'Maykes yow ashaymed, thass the wust
of it … t'think weem framed by that cunt?'

'Ashaymed to be English, thass the wust,
I've got these Euro cards for the cunt,
y'know for is' phone?' *Two wenches*
shared a wry smile, a nod. 'E loves cantin'
'e'd even cant with the Iraqi.'

'E loves 'is cantin,
if ever there's a blether yed 'e's the wust.'
Crumpled bag of Euro cards examined by two wenches.
'So, these am for the Iraqi?'
'Naw, these am for that Tomo, the cunt!'

A wry smile, a nod between two callused wenches.
'Which one's the crack head then? Who's the wust?'
'Yom the wust, Swopson, blartin' like a cunt,
these are for Tomo, then 'e cor lamp anyone for cantin'.
Right, ready, let's go find the Iraqi.'

Tomo's Sonnet

That Tomo from Tipton was guilty, they said
'e's a sign-on scrubber and a blether-yed
who'd sell is' own mom for tuppence a crack,
an sell 'is own arse for a tewtree a smack.
Them the wust ferrit, them wammels, waggin'
on the box. Blartin' – while the UKs laggin'
behind Eastern reds, who'd tek all you own,
they'd slit you a new smile just for your phone.
It coulda bin the Imam from Lye Town – the one
that wrote them poems for 'is daughter and son.

Tomo is guilty, 'e went with a smile
and we, in our reaping, work on beguiled.

Wieland II

'E teks 'is embers up to bakers
an' they raise kin on risin' dough.
'E's tools for wounds an' judge to flakers
E' teks 'is embers up to bakers,

an' shares is flames wid glassmakers.
So above an' so below.
'E teks 'is embers up to bakers
an' they raise kin on risin' dough.

Agenoria

Ethereal footprints
built from blasts of glass-flame
and enveloping engine-rumbles
guiding our goods.
Stalking steel rails,
passengers
peeping forward – peeping back,
cut elements.
We are set to trail the freight
as it tutors sand to glass.
Actum Agenoria!
Here is the history we track.

The Cradle

During the day and during the night
fires on all sides light
the landscape in fiery glows –
constant twilight reigns.

Broken by hills
of cinders
the echoing green,
honeycombed
in mining galleries –
almost unknown ...
iss plastic an' electric light
that measures us now, ay it?

Forges pour plagues,
Cut-minerals mek
shot and cannon
for Colonel Dud,
to sink Charles' foes –
Thatcher fucked
the redbricked and hardskinned,
iss PPI an' empty pubs
in the sink 'oles now, ay it?

We play our part in sinkings:
anchors and chains
of ill-fated voyages
forged in the cradle –
where blind Gin 'osses
walk doleful rounds
passed houses
half swallowed in pits

and timber ribs
of half corpses.
We med worlds
of Cowboys and Indians
on tracks where
shoots pierce
rusts of sheet steel.

Slate grey bricks steam up over Stour,
nothing slips across Stambermill,
to Round Oak, Brierley Hill.
We exchange introvenous plagues
between arches now, doh we?
The moms doh know we goo theya.

Down in Ma' Pardoe's,
coarsely clad, they
converse in bleared oaths.
Weem looking forward – looking back,
weem stondin' still.

During the day and during the night
fires on all sides light
the landscape in fiery glows –
constant twilight reigns.

'E's took 'is eggs to a fine market, ay' 'e?

'E's took 'is eggs to a fine market, ay' 'e?
Thass 'ow it started as we all drapped cork-legged.
'E was bostin' as a bab,
bought me suck on our run owem,
lamped that lommock Baggins
who was big as a Bonk 'oss.
'E's took 'is eggs to a fine market, ay' 'e?

The estate closed when the Patent Shaft was pulled,
Soaked 'is severance baked on Batham's –
'is wench left after that.

Grinding jaws and
chewed down nails and
archives of old magazines,
the same old clothes and
stinky shoes and
the way 'e looked like 'e wanted to say *'ow do*,
but quickly turned away.

But 'e was always ivverin'
and ovverin' by the gates,
while we was busy mekin' chains
and thinkin' of ha'p'orth dates,
'E took 'is eggs and went werritin',
blartin' like a gleed under the door,
while we were aytin' Tetnul Dick
and starin' at the floor.

'E's took 'is eggs to a fine market
and we all drapped cork-legged
after that cork-winder 'e gid 'im.

Wieland III

'E'd gid yo' 'alf a anythin'
'e 'ad an' e could spare,
thass why the swan-wench fell fer 'im –
'e'd gid yo' alf a anythin'.

'E coked a feather into a ring
daiked with a Tetnall pear,
thass why the swan-wench fell fer 'im –
'e'd gid yo' alf a anythin'.

Versus

At fourteen
Dave King,
(just a bloke,
ran the High Street
sports shop,
married, supped a pint
and mowed the lawn
on a Sunday)
football manager,
became our hero.

Each week
Uncle Alan walked
me and Ashley
up to Lye Town FC.

Terraces stood
in corrugated rust
and stained concrete.
Twenty loyal fans
stood against
October breezes,
spaced out
along the touch,
each a stranger to each,
each leave wife alone, thankful
for ninety minutes peace,
each struggle
with closed steelworks,
with special brew,
with bookie receipts,
with Balti Bazzar standing
on the corner
where Bennet's Butchers was.
Collars turned up,

fists clasp polestyrene cups –
piss-tea steams faces.

> *See, at fourteen*
> *we'd moved in*
> *to a new build home*
> *and down there*
> *people had golf clubs*
> *in their double garage*
> *and tipped their wage*
> *on Waitrose dinners.*

Mud patches
on faint grass
stood as pitch.
the air –
sweat, damp dirt, bovril.

And despite this
site of par-boiled life
I loved it,
instantly.

By the first fortyfive
Stourport were
caining Lye three – nil.
The grey faced and grey haired
stood fast in stiff observations.

> *That darky can run, cor 'e?*
> Eyes roll, lips stay shut –
> *Bernie doh know better,*
> *besides, in 'is own way*
> *'e's bein' nice.*

See, at forteen,
mah mate, Syed,
a 'paki' from Lye,
was smart and tough
and stuck up for me an' Ash
and 'e played wing at lunch
'cause 'e 'ad a left foot on 'im,
but by sixteen, 'is colour and mine
were too much for 'im
and the others
who learnt to be versus.

I'm still not sure,
Eighteen years on,
If I should be cross.

King made substitutes –
Lee Booth on for Matthews.

Boothy was a bull,
never missed, shrugged
off players with
strong shoulder-butts –
a Black Country Cantona.

I 'eard Bob gorr'a kickin'
aartside The Shovel.

'E did, ar – bin fuckin' Sue, ay 'e?
ar'd a tore 'is fuckin' cock off!

See, at fourteen
our Ashley
took a lampin'
for fingerin'
Laura Cockburn
on the rec,

but 'er was with
Craig Smith,
who was solid –
and all of us just watched it 'appen,
and we was alright
but Craig Smith was a cunt
and built a versus for life.

I'm still not sure,
Eighteen years on,
If I should be cross.

Long ball to chest – faint left,
split the defence,
half-volley bolt
sticks the ball in the net –
three – one.
The pitter patter clap
of appreciative pensioners
and us.

Corner ball,
King's outta the dug,
Ashley blinks
as Boothy connects
head to swerving cross
and King goes mad,
and we go mad,
and Stourport are sinking.

That Paki can curl the ball, cor 'e?
Bernie again.

'E doh understand
'ow the old cobblers
can now be a cornershop
and home to ten kids
and they wo' tek 'is word
fer a pay ya Fridee.

See, at fourteen,
Syed was third Gen
British-Asian
and so were a third
of Redhill School
so we day see
no Enoch Powell
flood plains.
The cumin perfume
and brown flesh were
difference we were used to.

I'm still not sure,
Eighteen years on,
If I should be cross.

'Come on Lye Town' –
our twenty strong crowd
still snuggled
in winter coats –
each still a stranger to each,
each still half-werritin'
over tomorrow's bread –
the bladder deflects
from the centre-half's head
and Boothy sticks out
an instinctual left boot ...
'Off side!'
no flag, ref shrugs,
and the keeper smashes fists to soil,
and King smashes fists to air,
and we roar
at the three all draw
and the fight we saw
on that derelict lawn.

Uncle Alan walks us home,
the old timers
do the same –
grimaces tame slightly,
tame a short time,
for Boothy and the boys
had done enough
and Dave King
became our Brian Clough.

Lost documents

'is name was Boxer, I never knew why,
the old grenadier begins to try
to recall the thick fear humidity
of Kuala Lumpur turbidity,

where gunmen knew emergency
was just another word. Insurgents
squatting and ready in the jungle fen
tamed by the torture of their children –

but we doh talk of that, he carried
on with Boxer, who never tarried
through mire or fire. *He snapped images*
of any insect, plant or burned village ...

it was a bostin' camera, he shot
Sakai, Batek, MNLA. Got
us to watch 'is camera when out on
manoeuvres – feeding swamp bombs

to the hidden, waiting for the rash
race of indiscriminate bone ash.
But we don't talk of that, we never
dwell on those negatives. We tether

the developing to more tethers,
send an aid parcel in bad weathers
and shake off the campaign dust,
governing the way unnamed towns rust.

I'd told 'im no, Stan starts up again,
Wharr'if it broke or fell to the fen,
so 'e took it with 'im last time out.
Shot in the neck. We'd never learn about

what was behind the lens.

'E grew the best runners in Bilbrook

'E grew the best runners in Bilbrook,
always 'ad a grin an' an *'ow do, cock?*
always 'ad handshake
for stranger an' kin
an' e'd drive us mad with 'is cantin'
'e'd never leave anyone loney.

'E grew the best runners in Bilbrook,
'Stan's Patch' marked 'is plot
an' 'e marked plots with poppies
for 'is muckers who fell in Malaya,
an' 'e'd tell tall tales
of guardin' the palace
an' blartin' with the Duke
about cheeky ales
down the Bag O' Nails.

'An sometimes
with a bowl-gut a scotch
you'd 'ear 'im singin'
Johnny Cash laments
in slurred baritones.

When Nan an' Mom
went up the bridge
'E tipped me two fingers
of whisky an' said:
You know, our Rob,
me an' ya Nan, we always
say good mornin', every
mornin', thass right, that is.

'E grew the best runners in Bilbrook
an' 'e 'ad a jab to go with left hook
an' 'e beat back death in the jungle
an' 'e beat back death in a truck crash
an' I wish I could lay my knuckle
on that cruel, twisted curse
that steals minds before their time.
But I kip it locked in,
an' lock in
on 'ow even at the end
'e'd force 'is tired mouth to grin
at the sight and sound
of 'is great grandkids.

Wieland IV

'Er was sound an' 'e called 'er Feathers
an' 'er knew the score of 'is toil
so 'er day fuss with donnin' leathers.
'Er was sound an' 'e called 'er Feathers

an' 'er'd kip the fire gooin' through all weathers
an' er'd mek gems out the soil –
'Er was sound an' 'e called 'er Feathers
an' 'er knew the score of 'is toil.

Borderlands

'We're all Middle Class now!'
Lord Prescott

It's always been the borderlands –
borders we make, borders
put upon us
borders in the borders.

> Granddad holds forth about Kuala Lumpur conquests
> we've heard again and again. Nan does her duty.

> Old coals built them and their difference.

Stambermill viaduct divides his growth:
site of tissue bombs and resin bongs,
graffiti wars between Baggies and Wolves.
Looming grey bricks arch over plains
where the Stour cuts industrial estates
and municipal grasses where the kids,
whose Dads were on the box after Kuwait,
taught us porn and fags and illicit words.
We weren't quite as *working* as them –
didn't matter then.

> Paul moved south after Uni, *e' sez charnce and barth now,*
> *Linda told 'im – there ay an R in it, chance rhymes with pants.*

> Old coals burn in tongues.

The middle son boards
with Mother, she could tell a tale –
the only child of a factory wench
and ex-guardsman,
with council estate maisonette,
the stench of salted meats

and carbolic soap. Father,
eldest of three in Post-War Semi,
where tobacco, wine and classical
music steep the scene.
Watched his Mum die at seventeen,
never says a word about it.

Old coals, still subsiding.

Their spawn, treading waters.
Working enough for Pennfields,
Middle enough for Pedmore –
he ploughed a border. *Nah, 'e's alright,
'e knows Armitage but 'e'll gerr'on
the end of a cross with a minute of lunch
to spare.*

Madge,
who did her Tony Harrison thing,
said *a bit of honest vulgarity, better
than them imagined pretentions.*

Old coal gets a spit polish.

New builds and period homes mottled
the other side of Stambermill, where the wraith
of the viaduct is fogged. A grinning
perjurer declares *things can only get better.*

I doh like 'im, Nan says, *'e's an hyena.*
'Er was right.

Old coal, old oil, old game.

We had books,
Dad subscribed to Reader's Digest
and demolished lit for fun –
a big American firm took him on.
Mum had her trinkets –
corn dollies, porcelain mice –
cultured a supermarket into a classroom.

They had rows of Penguin books,
neatly aligned amongst black and white
family portraits and kitchens
of locally sourced goods.
Have you ever been anywhere outside Europe?
We weren't quite as *Middle* as them,
we noticed that then.

Eileen says

Eileen said –
Down in worcester, them posh down theya,
sound liyke farmers
and the wenches wear
coats med a' the sem stuff
as nan's threepiece.
The barrista couldn't understand
how 'er asked for *tay fer two –*
'er took me as saft, 'er did.

Eileen doh need 'em to know
how 'er yeds med
like Royal Brierley.

Bob the Fish

Windows steamed
with blinks of bitter exhales –
Bob breathes
like he drinks –
gulps in goldfish gasps,
gawps, doh say a word.
The old naval pugilist
teks 'is time over last 'alf
as 'is wench meks tay.

Down the Exchange
them baked on Batham's.
The players,
who skeleton
the pub daily,
pack up deck and crib board –
Cheers Bob, y'am a good'un.

> *'E's sound, our Bob,*
> *'e 'elps John,*
> *ya know,*
> *John with Parkinson's,*
> *'e 'elps 'im down*
> *the allotments.*

Ritual everyday,
bobs to and from the taps
to sup,
rolls slug sized cigarettes
wears filthy shorts
through autumn's bite.

Ernie studies the form –
Bob, the window.
They nod,
sit at opposite ends,
doh spayke
but exchange cards each Christmas.

> *'E paled that Polak*
> *next door, day 'e?*
> *Gid 'im a corkwinder*
> *wi' a 4×4,*
> *said 'e med too much noise,*
> *gorr'im right to the core.*

When young McKain's son
'ad 'is fust bab
everyone stuck a quid
in 'is collection.
Bob knew 'im as a nippa,
only tipped 'is glass.

Soul as grey as 'is 'air,
there's a Mild behind the bar
for tendin'
Leanne's baskets
when 'er was down in Burnham.
An' we all gerr'im one in
'cause 'e onny 'as two
before gooin' 'ome
to tend to mom.

We all come and goo 'ere,
slipping in and out
in our suppin'.

Between blinks,
I see
summat savage
oilslicked on iris.

Wieland V

Niohad was king, a new sort
an' e'd 'eard a Wieland's charms,
took 'is oss to Duddan Leah fort –
Niohad was king, a new sort.

Now our smith wor gerrin bought
an' Niohad day 'ave any qualms
Niohad was king, a new sort
an' e'd 'eard a Wieland's charms.

Sleepin' beasts

Skies mirror coal seams and slate of cinder smoke –
tethers grey birds to its oil slick,
cloaks wenches' washing lines,
hanging out failed whites
for blokes on the box
who doh know how to clear
the cloud in their eyes.

Down on The Wrenner land is littered –
winds clip used cans through estates,
passed scorched out sofas weedy teens
use to toll the day.
This land –
nesting tumour in a cold parish.

Iss like our Tim keeps cantin':
weem cut from 'ere in all iss umber,
like the cut was cut from clay.
We ay nature's sons,
just med of it, someway.
'Cause weem cut that way,
weem cut away.

Down on The Wrenner air is soiled
with unwashed pets, cigarettes,
dried booze, pizza crust breath.
This air –
pricked silica leak of rotting cells.

Tim treds the towpath to 'is ESA review,
over grit and sand 'e used to alchemy to glass
but now just plays a part
in weathering muck.

They doh know
wass under theya –
our earth's rotten
with trilobites.
Weem stompin' on sleepin' beasts.

Sam Said

Sam says,
I'm sick a the scabby 'ores,
all of 'em, spreadin' as 'e splits
'is wallet again.
Gorr'a be the big man, ay 'e?

Collier counts coins outloud,
does it down The Hope
each drunk Friday –
thass another six sheets this wik –
one wench'll always be around,
agree to tek 'im 'ome for it.

Sam says,
'e ay split a lip
since 'e was sixteen
an' they purr'im away for that.
Always the big man, ay 'e?

Collier cuts lips with fists,
does it down The Hope
each drunk Saturday –
there was three on 'em, Tom,
an' I wor stondin' for that.
Four or five fellas'll always be around
the sink 'oles of 'is tales.

Sam meks
Sunday dinner,
an' we all goo 'round,
an' nestle in 'er spine,
an' ignore each creak
of subsidence.

Collier chokes tar tears
that noose 'im to bed
each 'angin' Sunday –
yo' never did finish Mom's cracks
before 'er corked it –
digs those pits alone.

Fred Says

for Fred Swartz

Fred, from Philly, that other Penn, said
I don't dig what this Black Country is, man.
Black Country, who are you?
He'd read the ley lines of bell pits
and stared through the soot,
but he day know how bluecollar graft
an' faggots sat on the sem paths
as a pawn shop, Costa,
two fer one lunches,
To Let signs.
Thass just it, though, ay it,
weem the subsidence iss'self
an' what we lost is all we 'ave.

Ayesha's Sonnet

It ay a sodomy on Pope or Donne –
the rains on our plains am the sem
soiled bones of speech's skellington.
There ay a voice or sign without frayed hem.

Our Ayesha, 'alf caste, single mom
at teen, 'as more phil in 'er ken
than them teachers who *tsk* theya tongues.
'Er gorr'a fust class hons with eighty-seven

even though 'er's bin sin
shakin' 'er knickers at sad men
down The Crown. 'Er ay never bin
restin' in nettles – 'er grasps stems.

Your tongue ay worth a damn
When you say we ay nothin' but bibbles in a can.

Turn to them the other cheek also

Rousters on Clydebank,
Isle of Dogs or Albert Dock –
This fuck you's for you.

> *If you want to cut your own throat,*
> *don't come to me for a bandage.*
> That lady turned –
> 'er turned switches off.

Shippers of Belfast,
Portsea Wharf and Hartlepool –
This fuck you's for you.

Steelworking Smoggies,
Llanwern, Port Talbort, Sheffield –
This fuck you's for you.

> *It was treachery with a smile on its face.*
> *Perhaps that was the worst thing of all.*
> That lady turned –
> turned to the few.
> And we turned with 'er.

The potters of Staffs
and all Cornish Fishermen –
This fuck you's for you.

Saltlicked Humber boys,
Matchstick men of Salford Quay –
This fuck you's for you.

> *Of course it's the same old story.*
> *Truth usually is the same old story.*
> They turn –
> and we turn with 'em.

Coalfields of Hatfield,
Thoresby, Selby, Cumberland –
This fuck you's for you.

> *In tough times,*
> *everyone has to take their share of the pain.*
> *The facts of life are conservative.*

Imagist in Netherton

So much depends upon
This is Art, spraycanned
on the redbrick shed
of the MEC
down in the maze
of Sledmere estate.

Cradley Haiku

Heath's filthy fetters,
bracing the edges of us –
Unify. Enslave.

Wieland VI

Our Feathers got speared an' plucked
Our Wieland got strapped to an' oss
I swear down yo'll get fucked,
now Feathers is speared an' plucked!

An' the king watched the township destruct
An' loffed at their furnace loss
As Feathers got speared an' plucked
An' Wieland got strapped to an' oss.

Pass Over

Occasional clink-squalls of metal on metal, the tram whispers
over bogs of lichens and mosses where ruins of factory tracks
sit between chewed up cars, withered rusts of dying foxgloves,
terraces and red brick mills. Now Garden City Hotspots
where artisans turned toil to song – home to meets
where eager eyes were braced for its own sake.

Now, *my marketing company work from a barn,* new media bred
from nouveaux riche neighbourhoods, riddled with stainless steel
and glass, faux plants and tokens of trade, *my bluechipped barn
farms consultants for consultants and cuntsaltonts and ...*

In the distance the unseen lungs of the basin bubble in the
matchstick models of crisscross waterways. Where Chance
Glassworks followed the ebb and flow, where grit from four corners
passed Galton Bridge, where rumbles clap an undercurrent, where
a 'proper pub' serves its scotch eggs with balsamic dressing to
twenty-four hour lawyers.

Wagtail

Chess sets
down on the cut,
the molten marble
black and white
ignores swarms
of dog-walking
families with
riling babs,
up a height over
by the bonk –
mother cantin':
boys am different, they just am
but them Muslim boys am even more, ay they?
A child, too young to know, nods along.

Tail feathered,
Playing black-white salutes
wagging, hopping –
black and white.
White on black, skipping
along the mud –
ochre clay
stains its veins.

Weem the rust pot of strange solutions.

Pigeon

A slate coat against grey time:
church spine,
littered with dumpy torsos
sat in line
to taste the morning
with the curtsy of tails,
agreements nodded out
like semaphores.

Sally stumbles
into the kitchen, still half asleep.
They nod their own semaphore –
she knows he's been at it again,
the next day was a goodbye note –
she couldn't help her slight smile.

Plump plumes on brittle sticks
jostle for a view. There is emerald
in the slate –
a tiptoe hop sends them soaring:
Awkwardness razed.

Herring Gulls of Gornal Wood

Territory echoes in a coop-caw chorus,
clattering terrace rows
as machinists break fasts,
hectic parents scrum passed
speckles of teenage barks,
baby squawks. The coop-caw rasps
in snare drum claps – a guttural kaa-kaa
over this morning's scraps. Raptored beak –
yoked with blood spot – snaps to yodel leftovers,
snaps to strike at smugglers
trying the same game.

> *Why am they called Seagulls, Mom,*
> *when we ay by the sea?*
> *Should call 'em Gornal Gulls.*

The neighbour no one speaks to
wrestles through the dew
to the recycling bins,
pitched on the car park
where teens spit and swear
at the lack of new models –
'E's bin pickin' on little Sammy,
'Er's bin pickin' over glossy bones of celeb mags –
the neighbour no one speaks to searches for plastic intimacy.

Soon, taupe spans
soar to another spot – do it all again.

Bren says

Bren said,
Liberal ay spaykin' to know one bur'imself
an' it ay nothin' more than empty signs
when 'is yappin'. A choir of stitched lips
praise East Side Lattes and call
the brooms of 2011 cleanups
a revolt...
Thass 'ow they took
everythin' but the gates from the forge,
the doors of Walsall Library,
Dawn's DLA
without a bite from us.

Fists unfurled
to pat
at backs –
a pack
of stitched lips.

Wieland VII

Duddan Leah died from the freeze –
It doh tek long for embers to cool,
now all you 'ear is a breeze.
Duddan Leah died from the freeze.

Niohad'd done it with ease –
taught the kin to play the fool.
Duddan Leah died from the freeze –
It doh tek long for embers to cool.

Call Centre Operative Achieves Satori

At Nine Locks Scrappy
I sid maggots
over a badger's carcass,
shed silica
an' become flies.
We was kids,
we day know nothin'
was comin'.

Well done you! Yawping
at new found competence –
and I just smiled, shrugged
a faux-modesty, continued
mapping χ to another function.

No really, iss really good, you've done really good.
The certificate on my desk, eye catching,
as I blankly take inanimate files and blankly
sentence them to inanimate stores where Spheroplasts
quiver – barely together. *'E's competent now, Phil.*

Phil notes with wild eyebrows –
I'm struck mapping χ to another function –
it'll make his next team huddle
where our readiness is stricken
by plastids and conjugation
bears.

At Nine Locks Scrappy
I sense bluebottles being
pulled back into pupa,
at my desk I am
mapping χ to another function.

Merry Hill

From the remains of Roundoak
(still warm before rust)
buds the cenotaph –
a hankersore,
sharp, sanitised
with slick polish.

Instead of taming steel,
that feeds every chink
of our honeycomb,
we're sold xenos
that breed skulkworms
over our loot.
They chew
and mottle lavea
through our roots.

Ikea Sunset

Flat packs cast jet blacks –
despite de stijl shades
of Bauhaus shelves –
over James Bridge,
where the to and fro
of traffic slipstreams
an old town's blisters –
·commuters' eyes shift
in split seconds
between M6 lanes,
MPH, half-drained coke can
and this slick span of retail.

Home for Bank Holiday –
I've been meaning to get that
faux thirties sideboard – ooh my coke –
to finish off the study – 87 miles to Liverpool –
and there's still the carpets to pay for –
better put foot to floor.

Pacing the market,
Bren glares at the passing,
passes The Bellwether –
there's no alms for his Bitter, no more –
he'll take milky tea with Sid
at the slag of Priory food bank.

'Ow do Sid, Crucible still burnin'?
Still a few embers, our Bren. Yo'?
Lickin' the lid a life, me mon...
...what we got fer scrap today?

Seb and Grace
talk colour schemes
on plastic chairs
over swedish meatballs.
Their dollar-dollar-bricolage
has redefined 'craft'.

It's refined –
an alloy of ruin.

Sid skulks back
to Friar Park,
counts the quids
left in 'leccy and gas,
dreams of days he won
the hundred yard dash
at the sports day
for Patent Shaft.
Bren's the same –
see that sleepy-shiver-twitch –
as you pass by
James Bridge.

Shut yo' gob

Shut yo' gob
with Aynuk-Ayli tales
we know the loff
of 'ow they mistook
salt for kaylie
an' 'ow weem solute
to theya solvent.

Tell it to John
an' 'is single mom
where there ay nothin'
but the glue
an' markin' tracks.
'Is mon 's gone
an' Mr Smith day
act on 'is ADHD
an' there ay a wench
who'd tek on a jitterer,
an' no toil for a wazzock.

All 'e's got 's 'is front,
an' yo' wan'im to loff?

Shut yo' gob.

Our End

Adam loved it down our end.
We 'ad vhs an' betamax
an' went to Nan's caravan
every 'alf term, an' we 'ad
belly draft which wor a posh cut
then, an' Dad took us to Judo
on a Fridee, an' our Shell did tap,
an' there was woods at the back
of the 'ouses where wid play
cowboys, an' there was that one time
wid found a porno an' I was too young
to know, an' we did rope swing over
the Stour until the Quarry Bank gang
turned up, then it'd be back to Dean's
an doh tell the moms but we watched
Raw'ead Rex while they was out drinkin'
cider on the drive, an' if it ay rainin' tomoz
I'm racin' Paul down Graylin' Road
but I'm lerrin 'im win 'cause Louise is watchin'
an' the boys know but the wenches doh.

Adam loved it down our end
'cause 'e day 'ave any brothers an' 'is 'ouse
was up by all the olduns, like Wendy an' Frank,
who never gid our balls back,
'is dad'd sin stuff in Bosnia
'is mom 'ad a gammy leg.
Adam'd get excited an' wid end up
in the shit with someone, but we was a gang
an' you day grass (an' ya still doh).

Andy wor part of it, 'e come from Lakeside
an' day get 'ow you got by
with only last year's mega-drive,
an' I think thass why 'e grassed
years later, after 'e took the piss outta
Dipak for 'avin' Hi-Tech trainers,
Dipak struck back,
'is brother'd bin a boxer
so 'e knew to kip arm relaxed an' fist tight,
it took Andy by surprise,
but somehow it day learn 'im.

Adam loved it down our end.
'Is mom was older than ours
so 'e'd do the shop each wik
an' it was in the frozen isle
with a pork joint in 'is 'onds
when Andy thought 'e was a pushover
an' med a deal out of 'is everyday beans
an' savers flakes, an' sheets a coupons.

Adam loved it down our end.
Our Manda looks out for 'im now
as 'er locks up cells
at HMP Featherstone.

09:00, Victoria Square, Brumajum

The way upward and the way downward is one and the same

Call centre insects
queue for caffeine
minutes before stint.

      And the pool was filled with water of sunlight,
      And the lotos rose, quietly, quietly

The museum's browncoat
studies his – he has time to steep –
his shifts am slashed.

      And they were behind us, reflected in the pool.

Sat, between commerce and art,
where TS Eliot lines a yorkstone pond,
with hangover coffee, staring at the floor.

Weeds peep through paving cracks.
Leftovers litter me.

      The surface glittered out of heart of light,

Right – a discarded paintbrush.
Left – a used condom.

Iss odd,
what walls
our oikos.

      Then a cloud passed, and the pool was empty

Wieland VIII

Case hardened, spends daylight 'ommerin' the bloom,
hamstringed, in the smithy of the king –
Iss gonna be 'is tomb.
Case hardened, spends daylight 'ommerin'. The bloom

'e spies is 'is own slow doom –
'e's forged 'is trade mekkin' rings,
case hardened. Spends daylight 'ommerin' the bloom.
Hamstringed; the smithy of the king.

The Wedlac

for Amanda and Kyle

Up on Brierely Bonk,
where the'd pledge
sand an' flame to glass,
two others med a troweth –
one wench, one mon
an' four words:
Ah love yo', bab.
Thass the burnt ring
a wedlac 's med.

See down in 'agley
or Kiddi, or Penn
they'd think the Delph
wor nothin' but the cut,
strange folk in strange pubs,
the filth a' nine locks scrappy
but this wench an' this mon know
'ow Brierley Bonk
etches shell-thin crystal
from iss muck.

Thass why
it day matter
'ow our Kyle
took to 'is knee
on the car park concrete
with 'is infectious grin,
solemnly asks:
Will yo' marry me, Mand?
an' 'er day 'esitate,
an' 'er smiled back
with broad, wild gob –
Yes, 'er sez.

Up on Brierely Bonk,
where the'd pledge
sand an' flame to glass,
two others med a troweth –
one wench, one mon
an' four words:
Ah love yo', bab.
Thass the burnt ring
a wedlac 's med.

Them the fire an' sand
tutored to cut-glass –
raw, corporeal, lush –
like their love.

I lost my heart to a Delph Run wench

Sure,
'er's got pink lips
an' slick limbs
an' 'er does more,
by ten, for others
than 'erself,
but iss more about
'ow 'er eye looks
when 'er suddenly
stops on page 98
of 'er latest thriller
wi' a yawp – iss the brother!

Sure,
'er's a lay, fuck is 'er a lay,
'er's a sort, an' wo' let mates
goo short, goo home alone,
goo lonely. 'Er works wi' mongs,
but iss more about
'ow 'er knows makaton
for 'cunt' an' uses it on club
dance floors full of indie-girls.

Sure,
'er's got umber eyes
an' ashen flesh
an' bitch howl curves
but iss more about
'ow 'er joined
in, mekin' up a story
wi' me, 'bout the kid
in the bar, with his
top-knot dreadlock,
flipflops, sat cross-legged
on 'is aged armchair

dippin' gluten free crusts
into organic gazpacho.
'Er turned
'im into an 'orror story –
told us 'ow 'e'd done
Asia an' done Australia
an' done school buildin'
in Kampala. 'Ow 'e'd bin
to old plantations in Guyana,
an' cordycep spores
dusted 'is hair, burrowed
like John Hurt's parasite,
punctured trachea,
bust up jugular.
'Er med this up wi' me
over too much wine
one night in Torquay
an' thass why.

Sure,
'er's got 'er tongue studded
an' 'er legs wrapped around
my frame are softer, safer,
sexier than anywhere.
'Er gid a homeless mon
a fiver once,
mainly 'cause 'e 'ad a dog,
an' 'er grins when 'er farts
an' 'er's like me an' we doh eat meat
an' we dance in empty rooms.
But iss more about
'ow 'er voice raises
when 'er spies novelty teapots
in charity shops.

Iss all a me delph wenches things
but, sure,
iss the odd, small, things
I could weep over.

Litter

Sometimes smashed glass,
scattered on asphalt
outside a pub,
is a constellation.

Acknowledgements

Thanks are due to the editors of the following publications where some of these poems were first published: *Black Country Broadsheet, The Black Light Engine Room Press, Envoi, Agenda, The Fat Damsel, Raum, Prole, Anti-Heroin Chic, Euonia Review, Three Drops From a Cauldron* and *A Swift Exit*. Thanks also to the editors of the following anthologies: *Poetry of the Black Country* (Offa's Press) and *Spake* (Nine Arches Press); poems in this collection found home in their pages.